LIFE CYCLES

Frog

Ruth Thomson

D1324144

Explore the world with **Popcorn** - your complete first non-fiction library.

Look out for more titles in the **Popcorn** range. All books have the same format of simple text and awesome images. Text is carefully matched to the pictures to help readers to identify and understand key vocabulary.
www.waylandbooks.co.uk/popcorn

Published in 2013 by Wayland

Copyright © Wayland 2013

Wayland
Hachette Children's Books
338 Euston Road
London NW1 3BH

Wayland Australia
Level 17/207 Kent Street
Sydney NSW 2000

Managing Editor: Victoria Brooker
Concept designer: Paul Cherrill

British Library Cataloguing in Publication Data:
Thomson, Ruth
 Frog. - (Popcorn: Life Cycles)
 1. Frogs - Life cycles - Juvenile literature
 I Title
 571.8'1789

ISBN: 978 07502 7204 9

10 9 8 7 6 5 4 3 2 1

Printed and bound in China

Wayland is a division of Hachette Children's Books,
an Hachette UK Company.
www.hachette.co.uk

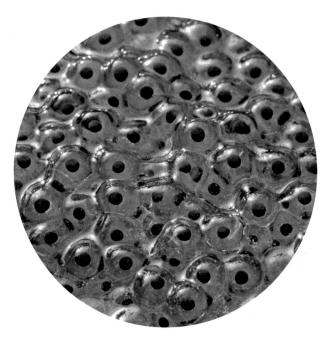

Photographs:
Cover, 15, 16 Robert Pickett/Papilio; 2, 12, 13, 14, 17, 18, 19 Photolibrary group; 4/5: Ian West/Photolibrary Group; 6 Imagebroker/Photolibrary Group; 7, 9, 22 NHPA/Photoshot; 8 © Jean Hall/Cordaiy Photo Library Ltd./CORBIS; 10 London Scientific Films/Photolibrary Group; 11 David Boag/Photolibrary Group; 21 Woodfall/Photoshot

Contents

Frogs gather

It is spring. Frogs gather at the pond where they were born.

How many frogs can you spot?

The pond is a noisy place.
The male frogs croak
to attract a female.

Frogspawn

Each male sits on a female's back and grips her tight. She lays hundreds of eggs which he covers with a liquid from his body.

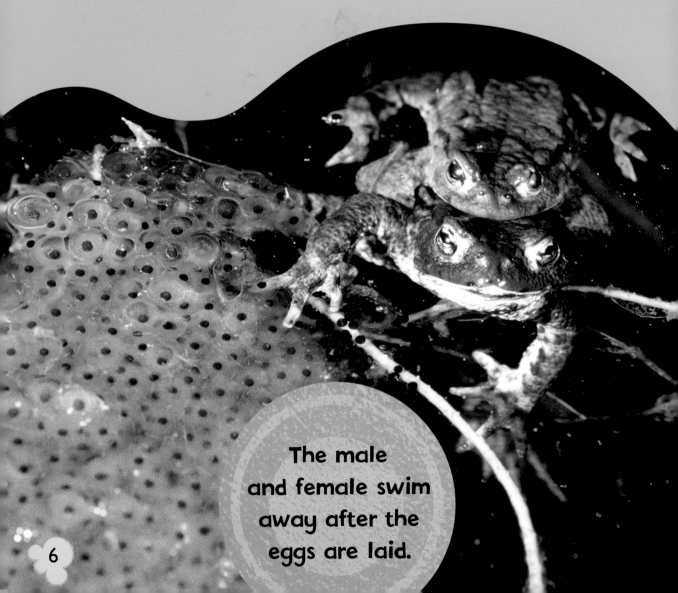

The male and female swim away after the eggs are laid.

Each egg is safe inside a clear
jellyball. The eggs stick together
in a group called frogspawn.
They float on top of the pond.

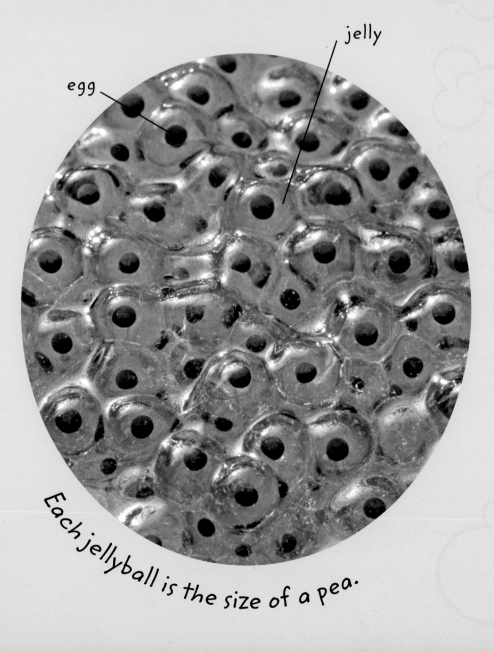

jelly

egg

Each jellyball is the size of a pea.

Time to hatch

The eggs change shape. They grow longer. After about ten days, they become tadpoles.

Can you see both the tadpoles' head and tail?

The tadpoles begin to hatch.
They wriggle out of their jellyball.
Then they stay together,
resting on the jelly.

Tadpoles

Young tadpoles nibble tiny plants.
They breathe with the feathery gills
on each side of their heads.

2
weeks

The tadpoles grow longer.
Their feathery gills disappear.
They breathe with gills inside
their body instead.

How does a tadpole swim?

 # Food

As tadpoles grow, they start eating tiny flies and water fleas. Tadpoles eat dead worms and fish, too.

4 weeks

These tadpoles are sharing a dead worm.

Fish and bigger insects, like this
dragonfly larva, eat the tadpoles.

Legs grow

The tadpole grows long back legs.
Its feet are webbed.

7 weeks

Why are webbed feet good for swimming?

Two shorter front legs grow.
The tadpole grows lungs instead
of gills. It comes to the surface
of the pond to breathe air.

9 weeks

# Froglet

The tadpole's tail shortens.

Its eyes bulge. Its mouth widens.

It grows a tongue. It is now a froglet.

12 weeks

Soon the froglet's tail will disappear. The froglet climbs out of the pond.

15 weeks

Fish, snakes and birds eat tiny frogs.

Frog

The froglet slowly becomes an adult frog. It lives in damp places. Its blotchy skin makes it hard to see. It eats insects, worms, slugs and spiders.

What is this frog eating?

The frog jumps from place to place
on its long back legs. It may dive
into the pond to escape hungry birds
and grass snakes who want to eat it.

Winter and spring

A frog cannot keep warm in cold weather.
It finds a safe hiding place for winter. It goes
into a deep sleep called hibernation.

A frog does
not eat or
drink during
hibernation.

When frogs are two years old,
they are ready to find a mate.
In spring, they go back to their pond.

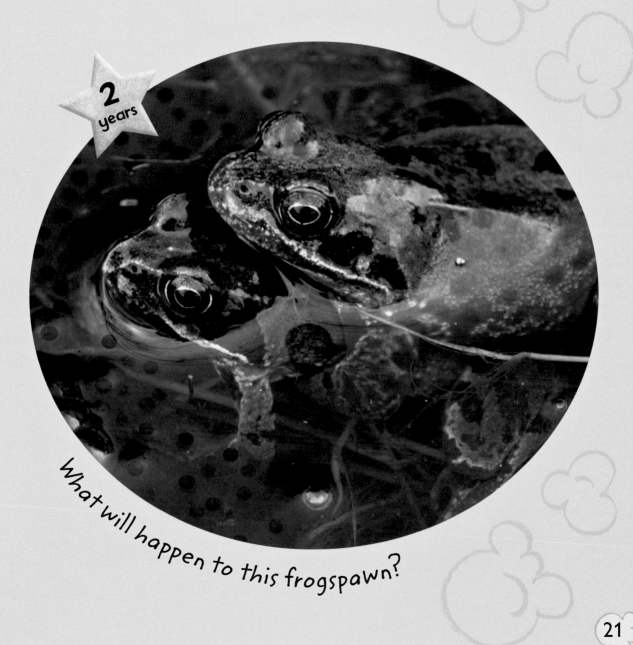

2
years

What will happen to this frogspawn?

Frog life cycle

In spring, female frogs lay frogspawn. The frogspawn grows into tadpoles. The tadpoles become froglets and froglets become frogs.

frogspawn
Female frogs lay eggs called frogspawn.

tadpole
Each egg hatches into a tadpole.

frog
The froglet becomes a frog.

froglet
The tadpole grows back legs then front legs and becomes a froglet.

Make a pop-up card

Make a funny pop-up frog card to surprise a friend or someone in your family.

1. Fold the paper in half widthways to make a crease. Open it out. Now fold it in half lengthways.

2. Cut a slit through the folded paper beneath the crease, as shown.

3. Bend both corners of the slit into triangles.

4. Fold the paper into a greetings card.

5. Draw grass on the front.

Who is hiding in the grass?

6. Draw a big frog face inside, with the creased slit as its mouth.

23

Glossary

croak to make a deep harsh sound

female a girl frog

gills part that a tadpole uses to breathe underwater

hatch to come out of an egg

larva an insect in its first stage after hatching

lungs part of the body that animals use to breathe air

male a boy frog

mate the male or female partner of an animal

webbed feet feet with skin stretched between the toes

Index